jmn

W9-BMV-657

Poems About FRIENDS

Kids Express

BY **America's Children**

EDITED BY Jacqueline Sweeney

BENCHMARK BOOKS

MARSHALL CAVENDISH
NEW YORK

For Emil D'Onofrio, my dear friend and fellow pilgrim. J.S.

The publisher and editor would like to thank the following schools for opening their doors to us: Alden Place and Elm Drive Elementary Schools (Millbrook Central School District), Amenia and Millerton Elementary Schools (Webutuck School District), Barnum Woods Elementary School (East Meadow Union Free School District), Beekman, LaGrange, and Noxon Road Elementary Schools (Arlington Central School District), Boght Hills and Blue Creek Elementary Schools (North Colonie Central School District), Carrie E. Tompkins Elementary School (Croton-Harmon School District), Central Avenue Elementary School (Mamaroneck Union Free School District), Gardnertown Fundamental Magnet School (Newburgh Enlarged City School District), Germantown Central School (Germantown Central School District), Hackley School, Pawling Elementary and Middle Schools (Pawling Central School District), Scotchtown Avenue School (Goshen Central School District), Tesago Elementary School (Shenendehowa Central School District)

And with thanks to the art teachers (who worked so hard and were so wonderfully supportive): Christine MacPherson, Mary Molloy, Leslie Ann Pesetzky, Carole Pugliese, Mitchell Visoky, Nancy Woogen, Kerry Yankowich, Ilga Ziemins-Kurens

Special thanks to: Miriam Arroyo, Barbara Bortle, Ellen Brooks, Angela Butler, Pat Conques, Dotti Griffin, Anahid Hamparian, Peggy Hansen, Sandy Harvilchuck, Naomi Hill, Carol Ann Jason, Jennifer Lombardo, Mary Lynne Oresen, Joanne Padow, Carol Patterson, Theresa Prairie, Tracy Racicot, Ellen Ramey, Linda Roy, Nicole Sawotka, Jude Smith, Faye Spielberger, Bev Strong, John Szakmary, Glen White, Mary Ellen Whitely

Benchmark Books
Marshall Cavendish
99 White Plains Road
Tarrytown, NY 10591-9001
www.marshallcavendish.com

Text copyright © 2003 by Jacqueline Sweeney
Illustrations copyright © 2003 by Marshall Cavendish Corporation

Book design by Anahid Hamparian

Library of Congress Cataloging-in-Publication Data

Poems about friends by America's children / edited by Jacqueline Sweeney.
    p. cm. -- (Kids express)
Summary: Poetry and art by children describing their feelings about friendship.
    ISBN 0-7614-1506-8
    1. Friendship--Juvenile poetry. 2. Children's poetry, American. 3. Children's writings, American. [1. Friendship--Poetry. 2. American poetry. 3. Children's writings. 4. Children's art.] I. Sweeney, Jacqueline. II. Series.
    PS595.F74 P64 2002
    811'.6080353--dc21
                    2002002201

Printed in Hong Kong
6 5 4 3 2 1

—Soren Dudley, *grade 2*

Contents

Teacher's Note

Imagine a classroom full of elementary school children bursting into applause upon hearing an announcement of an upcoming activity. Recess? Lunch? No. Writing poetry! Year after year, this is Jackie Sweeney's effect on students. I have been fortunate enough to witness this phenomenon over the last six years, as Jackie has conducted poetry residencies in the Arlington Central School District.

I study her as she teaches, trying to analyze her strategies. Although I have learned a lot from doing so, there is also some kind of magic at work here. Jackie is a modern-day alchemist, helping students turn their writing into something quite extraordinary.

What does she do? First, she convinces students that they are safe and their ideas are exciting. She focuses on free verse, providing structures through which she introduces students to poetic techniques such as sensory imagery, simile, metaphor, personification, and diction. At the same time, she invites students to surprise her with their own interpretations of these structures. She models extensively with examples from her own imagination and from the work of other students. Her samples are carefully chosen to counteract the notion that poetry treats only butterfly wings and flowers; topics range over every possible subject, from slithering pythons to pestering siblings.

Sensory perceptions are combined in surprising ways. Jackie might begin by asking students to picture a certain color and let it make them feel cold or hot or cool or warm. This is quickly developed into simile as she asks the students to consider how the color (let's say "red") is hot "like what?" As the students come up with their first tentative similes, Jackie immediately gets them to elaborate by asking questions until the child has produced: "Red makes me feel hot like a tomato on a white plate on a picnic table with the sun beating down on it on a summer day." Jackie exclaims, "Now I can see it!" and we are off on another year's excursion into poetry.

Peggy C. Hansen
Noxon Road Elementary School
Poughkeepsie, New York

Best Friends

When I am happy
I feel like I am best friend
to the whole world.
And I am.

—Marissa Kleiner, *grade 2*

The biggest thing in the world is my friend's
SMILE

—Arty, *grade 2*

—Jiyoung Kim, *grade 5*

The Gold Necklace

I believe that the most precious
things in the world are friends. Friends
hook on in massive chains like sparkling gold
necklaces. Sometimes one or two of the
connecting hoops falls off, but most of
the time you're given more.

If you lose a friend, you cannot
force her to like you. Friends are
delicate like glass sculptures.
If you make a wrong move
or say a wrong word,
you could break their
heart. Friends are like heavy
brown boxes labeled "fragile."

When I almost lost two
priceless gold hoops, I locked
myself in the bathroom, cried
for 15 minutes, and then went
to talk to my close friends.

Sometimes a kindred friend
is not good, because it makes
the chain loosen, and some
hoops fall off. The things
I treasure most are friends.

—Erika Gerstenberger, *grade 5*

Shadow Is My Dog

I love the name "Shadow."
Shadow is my dog. He
is black and white. Shadow
is hot like sparks. Shadow
is cold like ice.

"Dog" spelled backward
is "god."
Shadow is my brother.

—Kurt, *grade 3*

—Evie Grainger, *grade K*

Harry

Harry, you are the burst of an erupting volcano in Hawaii at the time the sun is up. You take me to a place where boys drive girls crazy every day. Harry, you are a massive blizzard that consumed the town of Pawling at night. You are also a hurricane in the state of New Jersey, but on top of it all, you are Harry Brockoff, my friend.

—Patrick Callan, *grade 3*

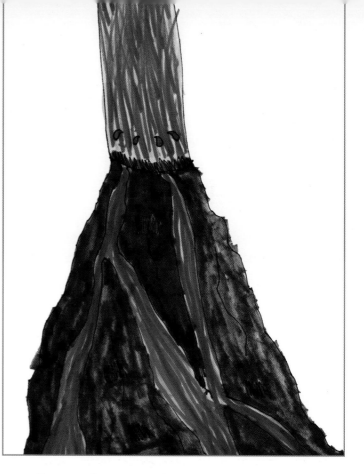

—Kyle Conkins, *grade 5*

The Smelliest Thing Is Adam's Fart

Adam's fart smells very bad. It shines like a brand new car. Adam's fart sounds like a hundred ducks. It makes the biggest sound. I could use Adam for a gun. He could use his fart. I'd probably die too. It really smells! I wonder how he does it. His fart is worse than my dog's fart, and my dad's. It goes as fast as a shooting star or a shooting gun. It almost killed me. It's too smelly for me.

—anonymous, *grade 3*

—Kathleen Otway, *grade 3*

Sadness

It takes a while
to go away.
My feelings
are hurt,
sadness bubbles.
My friends try
to comfort me.
It's no use.
My feelings are hurt.

—Katie Mekeel, *grade 4*

Kayla Kayla

Kayla Clapper is like a cat
wrapped in a blue blanket
in a brown basket. Kayla
Kayla, when you play soccer
you are like the wind that blows
in my backyard. Kayla, you are
like a flower in summer
that is blue. You are my
friend. Even though we
fight sometimes, you are
like the sun.

—Heather Knapp, *grade 2*

—Jill K. Daddona, *grade 4*

Friendship Is Good

When I'm left out
I feel like an ant
that died a long time ago. I
feel like I did something wrong
and they do not like me
so I walk away. I think
they hate me.
So I say if you think friendship
is good, you're right. If you
thing it's bad, you're wrong.

—Jacob Kartiganer, *grade 2*

I feel like a race car who just
got crashed up. I don't think there
is a color to show how
embarrassed I am. The other day
I fell in a hole outside. I fell
and started to cry. Everyone thought
that I was a baby. I ran to play
with someone else—someone
who won't pick on me.
Someone nice someone kind someone
like a best friend.

—William McCoy, *grade 2*

11

The Special Place

My special place is
John Canale's bed. When I am
on the top bunk I believe I
am on an airplane soaring
through the air. Sometimes when
I am up there I pretend I
am on a parachute going
on a hundred foot drop in
Massachusetts. Sometimes
when I'm there I see clouds.
I wish I could live there.

—Kristen Scudieri, *grade 3*

—Jake Tuttle, *grade 3*

Scary

The scariest thing is when
your friend is sleeping over at
your house and you hear your heater
tick-tacking. It sounds like rats
scratching on your heater. You start
getting nervous and you feel all funky
inside. Then you tell your friend
about what happened. Then your
friend helps you go to sleep
by telling you it's only your
heater tick-tacking.

—Shane Lyle, *grade 3*

—Stephanie Bonifacio, *grade 3*

Left out makes you feel like a cloud with no rain left.

—Nicole Wadhwa, *grade 3*

When I'm embarrassed I feel like a clown that got invited to a birthday and everyone was bored.

—Jimmy, *grade 2*

—Julia Morrison, *grade K*

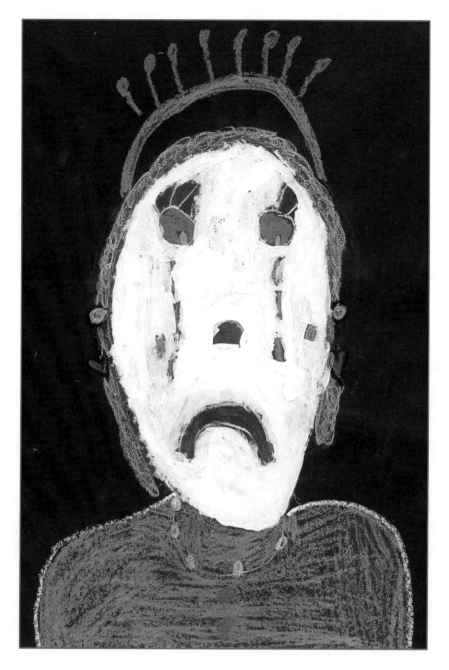

—Allison Flinn, *grade 1*

My Tears Tell a Story

Something sad has happened.
My grandfather has died. I hardly
remember him. It's like my memory
has been taken out of my head and
burned by a forest fire and all that's
left are ashes. The only thing I remember
is the cemetery where he was buried.
I try not to think about him.
If I do I cry. When I think about him
I know how my grandmother felt—
like you've lost half of your heart.
The only thing he is now is a
friend in my heart that I will
never let go.

—Zak Henry Bartholomew, *grade 2*

—Rachel Pierantozzi, *grade 4*

Being Weird

Being weird is hurtful inside
like needles pinning you
in a dark blue room and
it is cold and you are
crying.

When you were in a popular
world you had friends. Everybody
loved you. Then you found out that
they were only using you.

Now that they let you down you're
a dinosaur being killed by a raptor.
You can hear him ripping and munching
and crunching your tail and you know
that your life is going to end.

I am weird. I want to know why.

—Makaylla Bowdren, *grade 4*

—Marie, *grade 2*

17

—Dominick Anfiteatro, *grade 1*

—Ryan P. Clarke, *grade 1*

—Elyana Kadish, *grade 1*

—Kathryn Chamberlin, *grade 1*

My most frustrating day
was when no one
came to my birthday party.

—Andrew, *grade 3*

—Andrew Costa, *grade 3*

The most embarrassing day
was when my friends Danielle and
Amy told Nick that I liked
him so much. Even though
I do. My head was going
to explode.

I hate being in school now
because everyone is saying
"You like Nick, you like Nick."
I wish that day could start over.
I wish no one knew that
I liked Nick.

—Allison DeMuro, *grade 4*

Sad Feeling

My saddest feeling was when
my friends from a different
country moved back to
where they came from.
It felt like an ice cube was
going down my throat.

—Maria Smaldone, *grade 3*

Going Away

The saddest thing is when a friend
or someone in my family goes
away. The color of blue tears like
someone crying the waves
of the ocean. It sounds like a car or
a plane leaving to somewhere far.

My friend goes to another
school in Canada. He is
making friends now.

—Scott, *grade 2*

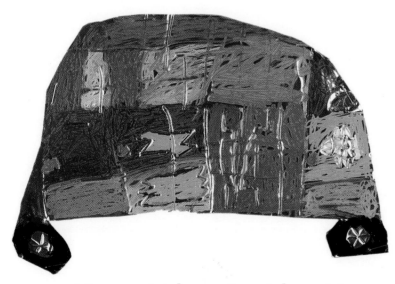

—Vincent Anthony Cacciola, *grade 2*

My heart is like

a loving hospital that

takes children who are hurt

and homeless.

—Lauren Fix, *grade 1*

—Christina Rossi, *grade 5*

Being Alone

When I'm alone
I feel like a raspberry
that nobody wants to pick.
I taste like a rotten
piece of potato, and
then I feel like a
tree that just fell.

Then I want to go to a world where
everybody is friends.
I want to
run and climb to
the top of a
tree and never
come down.

I feel like a cheetah
that can't even catch a turtle and
everybody calls me a
slowpoke. But one
day I'll catch a
friend.

—Tim Flynn, *grade 2*

—Rachel Pierantozzi, *grade 3*

23

When I'm Really Sad

When I'm really sad
I feel like no one likes me.
But one person likes me
and that person is Jennifer.
I like her. She's a girl.

—Jessica McGarry, *grade 1*

—Clare Wise, *grade 5*

Austin, you're like the red hot
sun, you're like the north star
leading my way to the future.
You're like the weather maker
that always brings sunny weather
to my house. It feels
like you're god controlling me
in the right sort of way. But,
you're the best in my eyes and
in real life. You are my
best friend.

—Shane Lyle, *grade 2*

When I'm happy

I feel like a flower
that people take good
care of and they water me
and I just start to bloom
in the air like a blue
tulip.

—Tzamira Cotton, *grade 2*

Blue Flower

Cheyenne is like a blue
flower just blooming.
Cheyenne makes
me feel good.
She was
blooming in Amenia.
When I am sad
I always pick a flower
and I pick her.
She makes me happy.
She is my best friend
my best best friend.

—Brooke Shaffer, *grade 2*

Jealous and Upset

When I was playing with my
best friend, the new girl asked her
if she could show her around
and my best friend said "yes."
I felt like whining and crying.
I felt so lonely and
so frustrated.
I kept on swallowing so
no one would know I
was crying. I went to
the bathroom and looked
in the mirror. I looked like
a weird person who
has no home.

—Ally Morrison, *grade 5*

—Jacob, *grade 3*

Why the Bus

My special place is on
the bus. My friends are
always there. We have fun.
On the bus it makes me
think what will happen when
I am older. Will I still
have the same friends?
Will some move away?
The bus sounds like a
frog's deep croaking. It smells
like cheese that's been in the
fridge too long. The bus sounds
loud like the city at noon.
The seats feel soft like my
feather bed. The bus is my
friend.

—Winona Mold, *grade 3*

—Hayley Lighthart, *grade 3*

My Happiness Place

. . . was my neighbor Palma's house in the Bronx.
I tasted cookies full of raspberry jelly with
chocolate on the bottom. I saw stems growing
out of the garden which grew into delicious
vegetables and beautiful flowers like
large fingers. I heard laughter when we were
together. I used to pretend that her house was
a planet and I explored looking for "aliens."
I always enjoyed going there even if
she didn't speak much English.
We understood each other
because we loved each other.

—Raymond Miller, *grade 5*

—Sean Roach, *grade 5*

When I Am Happy
I Feel So Good

When I am happy
I feel like a leaf
flying in the air and am going
to be found, going to be
kept. A little girl found me
and kept me and I felt good.
I made a friend for the first time.
Then she dropped me and a little
boy came and found me and
brought me home and he loved
me so much. We went to school
and everyone made friends with me
and loved me so much. He kept me
and one day his dad told him to
give me away—so he did. He gave
me to a girl and she kept me and
her mom liked me too.

—Madelaine Trotter, *grade 1*

—Amanda Coker, *grade 1*

Art credits

Author index

Squash like a Bug I am
I feel sad because I am
always left out of somthing
like I am a bug and then
all my friends get squashed
and then there is nobody to
play with.

I feel sad because I am
Lonely and I can't get
it out of my head and then
I feel like I can't get
along with the gang.

By Brandon mobley.

—Brandon Mobley, *grade 3*